HAUNTED AMERICA

——◆— A SPINE-TINGLING TOUR —◆—— OF AMERICA'S HAUNTED PLACES

by Matt Chandler and Suzanne Garbe

CAPSTONE PRESS
a capstone imprint

Haunted America is published by Capstone Press,
1710 Roe Crest Drive, North Mankato, Minnesota 56003
www.mycapstone.com

Library of Congress Cataloging-in-Publication Data
Cataloging-in-publication information is on file with the Library of Congress.

Editorial Credits
Anthony Wacholtz, editor; Heidi Thompson, designer; Marcie Spence, media researcher; Danielle Ceminsky, production specialist

Photo Credits
Alamy: Jeff Greenberg, 107, North Wind Picture Archives, 18; AP Photo: Lisa Poole, 26–27, Patrick Semansky, 9, Robert F. Bukaty, 21; Benjamin Jeffries: 48–49, 76–77, 77 Bottom Right, 78–79; Capstone Press: 65 Bottom; Cleveland Public Library, Photograph Collection: 64–65; Dreamstime: Robert Bleile, 24, Wangkun Jia, 22–23; flickr: Wayne Hsieh, 44–45, 47; Getty Images: American Stock, 70, Bettmann, 14–15, 71, 110 Top, 111, Flickr Vision/Steven Wagner, 42–43, George Rinhart, 99 Top, H. Armstrong Roberts/ClassicStock, 98–99, Lonely Planet Images/Stephen Saks, 40–41, Richard Cummins, 108–109, Richard Drew, 68, Visions of America, 52–53; Governor Sprague Mansion Museum, Cranston Historical Society, Cranston, RI, photo by Gregg A. Mierka, Artist/Historian: 30–31, 31 Bottom; Janice and Nolan Braud: 54–55; Library of Congress: 10–11, 17 Top, 19 Top, 24 – 25 Right, 28–29, 95 Bottom, 102–103, 110 Bottom; Newscom: Danita Delimont Photography/Alim Kassim, 113, Everett Collection, 95 Top, KRT, 14 Top, KRT/Mark Rightmire, 97 Right, Mark Washburn/MCT, 57, 58–59, University of Wisconsin-Superior KRT, 86 Bottom, 86–87, ZUMA Press/Earl Cryer, 100–101; NPS Photo: Mammoth Cave National Park Service, 50–51; Shutterstock: Alexey Kamenskiy, 104–105, Andresr, 88–89, 92–93, Chantal de Bruijne, Design Element, Cover Design Element, Dmitry Natashin, Design Element, Donald R. Neudecker, 94, echo3005, Design Element, elegeyda, Cover Design Element, gracious_tiger, 37, Ilya BIM, Cover Design Element, Ivakoleva, Design Element, John Brueske, 84–85, Jorg Hackemann, 36, Kelleher Photography, 12–13, littleny, 114–115, Map Resources, 116, 118, 120, 122, 123, MelBrackstone, Cover Middle, Nagel Photography, 4–5, nikkytok, Design element, Richard A McMillin, 32–33, Robert Kelsey, 96–97, STILLFX, Back Cover Design Element, Triff, 60–61, urbanlight, 38–39, Victorian Traditions, 11 Top, Zack Frank, Design Element; Svetlana Zhurkin: 16–17; The Grand Opera House: 74, 75; Tyler Bennett: 80–81 Background, 81; Wikimedia: MattHucke, 66–67, 73, The Authenticated History of the Bell Witch" published in 1894, 45 Bottom, 46, Mikefall2, 82–83, Redwoodperch, 69

Direct Quotations
Page 19: Jeff Belanger. "The World's Most Haunted Places." Rev. ed. Pompton Plains, N.J.: New Page Book, 2011, 108.
Page 21: http://hauntedlights.com/haunted1.html
Page 29: Michael Norman and Beth Scott. "Haunted America." New York: TOR, 1994, 133–134.
Page 39: Mary Beth Crain. *Haunted U.S. Battlefields.* Connecticut: Globe Pequot Press, 2008, 128–129.
Page 47: Troy Taylor. *The Haunting of America.* New York: Fall River Press, 2006, 224.
Page 55: Ibid., 176.
Page 58: Joanne Austin. *Weird Encounters.* New York: Sterling Publishing, 2010, 295.
Page 67: Brad Steiger. "Real Ghosts, Restless Spirits and Haunted Places." Detroit, Visible Ink Press, 2003, 355.
Page 73: "Lemp Stories." http://www.lempstories.com/textstories.htm
Page 83: "Ashmore—the Truth." http://blogs.wthitv.com/2010/10/29/ashmore-the-truth/
Page 98: Jeff Belanger. "The World's Most Haunted Places." Rev. ed. Pompton Plains, N.J.: New Page Book, 2011, 24.
Page 100: Ibid., 245.
Page 107: Ibid., 55.
Page 113: "Southwest Ghost Hunters Association." http://www.sgha.net/az/jerome/jeromegrand2.html

Printed and bound in China.
554570

HAUNTED AMERICA

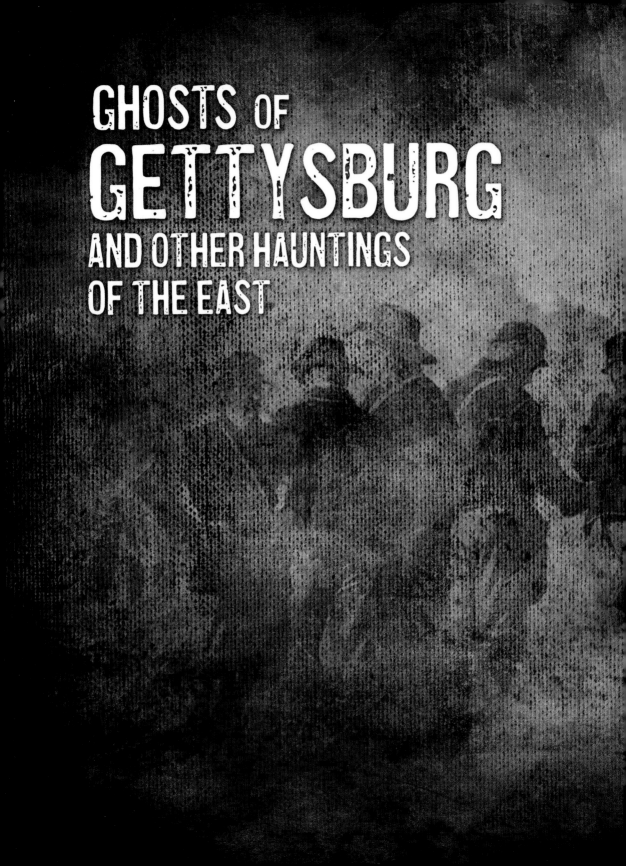

GHOSTS OF
GETTYSBURG
AND OTHER HAUNTINGS
OF THE EAST

TABLE OF CONTENTS

The eastern part of the United States is home to our country's oldest buildings and oldest recorded history. So it's not surprising that it's also home to some of our country's most haunted places. Scientists haven't been able to explain or prove the existence of **ghosts**. However, people throughout history have claimed to see ghosts and experience unexplained events. Get ready for a spine-tingling tour of some of the most haunted places of the East.

WESTMINSTER BURYING GROUNDS

One place said to be haunted is the Westminster Burying Grounds in Baltimore, Maryland. The famous American writer Edgar Allan Poe was buried there in 1849. Poe was known for his mysterious and creepy stories. After Poe died, people believed his ghost came back to haunt them. According to legend, Poe's ghost has been seen near his burial site. It has also been spotted in the **catacombs** beneath the cemetery.

Poe isn't the only ghost said to haunt Westminster. Visitors to the burying grounds have heard unseen children playing and seen a mysterious man in a gray vest. People claiming to be **mediums** have also heard a man yelling, "Go away!"

CITY: Baltimore, Maryland

FIRST REPORTED HAUNTING: unknown

TYPES OF ACTIVITY: ghost sightings, voices

SCARY RANKING: 2

ACCESS: Open to the public. Guided tours available, including a Halloween tour.

ORIGINAL BURIAL PLACE OF
EDGAR ALLAN POE
FROM
OCTOBER 9, 1849,
UNTIL
NOVEMBER 17 1875.

MRS. MARIA CLEMM HIS MOTHER-IN-LAW,
LIES UPON HIS RIGHT AND VIRGINIA POE
HIS WIFE UPON HIS LEFT UNDER THE
MONUMENT ERECTED TO HIM IN THIS

ghost—a spirit of a dead person believed to haunt people or places
catacomb—an underground cemetery
medium—a person who claims to communicate with the spirit world

GETTYSBURG BATTLEFIELD

The deadliest battle of the Civil War (1861–1865) happened in Gettysburg, Pennsylvania. As the **Union** and **Confederacy** clashed, more than 50,000 soldiers lost their lives over three days. The battle at Gettysburg was a blow to the South. Some people say soldiers who took part in the battle of Gettysburg still roam the battlefield.

CITY: Gettysburg, Pennsylvania

FIRST REPORTED HAUNTING: 1863

TYPES OF ACTIVITY: ghost sightings, strange smells, sounds such as footsteps and voices

SCARY RANKING: 5

ACCESS: The park is free and open to the public. Several private companies operate ghost tours.

Gettysburg has a long history of reported hauntings. The first one happened during the battle itself in 1863. During the battle, troops from Maine arrived outside of Gettysburg to support the Union. However, they weren't sure where to go. At a fork in the road, a man riding a horse and wearing a tri-cornered hat appeared. Hundreds of soldiers and several officers all said the figure had the face of George Washington. At the time, though, Washington had been dead for more than 60 years. Although startled, the troops followed Washington's directions. They arrived in time to help push back General Robert E. Lee's Confederate forces.

George Washington

Union—the northern states that fought against the southern
    states in the Civil War
Confederacy—the 11 southern states that left the United States
    to form the Confederate States of America

Civil War soldiers aren't the only people who have claimed to see ghosts at Gettysburg. Today the battle site is a national park. Many visitors claim to have had ghostly encounters. Some have seen a headless soldier riding a horse. Others have heard unseen babies crying and mysterious footsteps.

A monument in Gettysburg National Military Park honors Union Major General Henry Warner Slocum.

Some people think ghosts are reliving battle scenes of the war. Visitors have heard gunfire, running horses, and the heavy booms of cannon fire.

In one building during the war, injured soldiers' limbs were amputated and thrown out a window. Today a window in that building vibrates loudly.

One soldier is said to have haunted the cemetery for years. He was supposedly upset that his tombstone didn't mention the Medal of Honor he'd won. As soon as the marking was changed to include the medal, his ghost wasn't seen again.

LIZZIE BORDEN HOUSE

On August 4, 1892, the bodies of Andrew and Abby Borden were discovered in their home. Police thought they had been killed with an axe. Andrew's daughter, Lizzie, was accused of their murder. A jury found her not guilty, but people continue to debate whether or not she committed the murders.

Lizzie Borden

Today the house is a bed and breakfast and museum. Since it was reopened in 1996, guests have reported ghostly activities. Visitors have witnessed flickering lights and heard unexplained crying noises. Some have seen shoes moving on the floor without being touched. They've also heard screen doors slam, although the house has no screen doors. Some overnight guests report being tucked in by an older woman wearing traditional clothes. A housekeeper quit after she saw the imprint of a body in one of the beds.

CITY: Fall River, Massachusetts

FIRST REPORTED HAUNTING: 1996

TYPES OF ACTIVITY: ghost sightings, lights turning on and off, camera malfunctions, moving objects, sounds such as crying

SCARY RANKING: 3

ACCESS: The Lizzie Borden Bed & Breakfast Museum is open to the public.

THE WHITE HOUSE

CITY: Washington, D.C.

FIRST REPORTED HAUNTING: between 1852 and 1865

TYPES OF ACTIVITY: ghost sightings, footsteps, cold spots, strange smells, lights turning on and off

ACCESS: Free public tours are sometimes available.

The White House has been home to every American president for more than 200 years. The address 1600 Pennsylvania Avenue NW, Washington, D.C. is the most famous in the United States. But there's something else that isn't as well known about the White House—it may be haunted.

The first ghost reported in the White House was William Lincoln, Abraham Lincoln's son. William died of an illness in 1862. Abraham Lincoln's wife, Mary Todd Lincoln, claimed she saw the ghost of her son every night. He would stand at the foot of her bed and smile at her. Sometimes he came with other family members who had also died. Mary Lincoln told her half sister that seeing William's ghost comforted her.

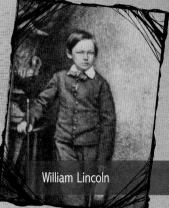

William Lincoln

However, not every White House ghost is as gentle. Some visitors have reported seeing the ghost of a British soldier carrying a torch. One couple said the ghost tried to set fire to their bed. Ghost hunters think it could be the ghost of one of the soldiers who burned down the White House during the War of 1812.

Dolley Madison

Dolley Madison's ghost is also said to roam the White House. The wife of President James Madison, Dolley was in charge of planting the White House's famous rose garden. One hundred years later, while Woodrow Wilson was president, gardeners were ordered to dig up the garden. According to legend, Dolley's angry ghost stopped the gardeners.

Other ghosts people have seen at the White House include former presidents Abraham Lincoln, William Henry Harrison, and Andrew Jackson. President John Adams' wife, Abigail Adams, has been seen hanging laundry in the East Room. Some people have said they could smell soap and wet clothes.

"When I turned the light on one morning, he [Abraham Lincoln] was sitting there outside his office with his hands over top of each other, legs crossed ... And when I blinked, he was gone."
– Tony Savoy, White House Operations Foreman

SEGUIN ISLAND LIGHTHOUSE

In the mid-1800s, a lighthouse keeper lived on Seguin Island, Maine, with his wife. His job was to keep the kerosene lamp lit so ships wouldn't crash into the land. The keeper and his wife lived alone on the small island. To keep his wife from getting bored during the long winter, the keeper bought her a piano. However, the piano had come with only one piece of music. The woman played it over and over, sometimes for hours at a time. Legend has it that the keeper was slowly driven crazy by the music. He took an ax and hacked at the piano. He then killed his wife and himself.

One hundred years later, lighthouse keepers began reporting eerie happenings. They saw doors slam and furniture move on its own. Some visitors claimed to hear the sounds of a piano playing in the distance.

In 1985 new technology allowed the lighthouse to run without a keeper living there. A crew came to clean out the house and remove the furniture. One crew member saw a woman's ghost appear at night. The woman said, "Don't take the furniture. Please leave my home alone!" The next day, they loaded the furniture onto the boat anyway. After everything was loaded, the engine suddenly stopped. The chain keeping the boat in place broke, and the boat sank.

CITY: Seguin Island, Maine

FIRST REPORTED HAUNTING:
1985, possibly earlier

TYPES OF ACTIVITY: music, noises,
ghost sightings, moving objects

SCARY RANKING: 5

ACCESS: The island is accessible only
by boat or helicopter; private ferries
are available.

"I heard a piano playing—a rather quick,
Scott Joplin style tune—I thought
perhaps it might be an unseen radio."
– a visitor to Seguin Island

1857

OMNI PARKER HOUSE

CITY: Boston, Massachusetts

FIRST REPORTED HAUNTING: 1941, possibly earlier

TYPES OF ACTIVITY: ghost sightings, moving objects, **orbs**, noises

SCARY RANKING: 3

ACCESS: The house is open to the public as a hotel and restaurant.

Guests and staff at the Omni Parker House hotel have reported strange happenings for more than 70 years. Guests have claimed to hear the creaking of a rocking chair, but the hotel doesn't have rocking chairs. A security guard once saw a shadowy figure in a stovepipe hat. Some guests claim the elevators go to the third floor without being called. Staff have also claimed to see orbs floating through the 10th floor hallway.

Harvey Parker, who opened the hotel in 1855, is the most widely reported ghost at the hotel. He worked hard to make sure his guests had an outstanding experience at the hotel and restaurant. Long after Parker died, his ghost was spotted on the 10th floor. Some hotel staff believe Parker stayed behind to make sure guests have a wonderful experience.

orb—a glowing ball of light that sometimes appears at a reportedly haunted location

COLONIAL WILLIAMSBURG

Williamsburg was founded in 1699 as the capital of Virginia. The city grew over time, but Colonial Williamsburg still exists. The historic area lies in the eastern part of the city. Some of the original buildings are still standing today, while others have been rebuilt. Some of the buildings, such as the Peyton Randolph House, are known for their ghostly history.

Peyton Randolph helped lead the Revolutionary War (1775–1783). He **inherited** his father's house, which was later named the Peyton Randolph House. Today the building is open to the public. Employees and guests have seen ghosts of women, men, and children in colonial clothing. The figures have disappeared right before the visitors' eyes. A woman who lived in the house in the mid-1900s also reported strange events. She claimed to hear footsteps and see the ghost of a teenage girl.

Raleigh Tavern is another site in Williamsburg where unexplained events have occurred. The tavern hosted dinners and parties for many people, including George Washington. Visitors to the tavern have heard the sounds of parties when no parties were happening. They have also smelled pipe tobacco when no one is seen smoking.

Raleigh Tavern

CITY: Williamsburg, Virginia

FIRST REPORTED HAUNTING: 1700s

TYPES OF ACTIVITY: ghost sightings, strange smells, strange noises and moaning

SCARY RANKING: 5

ACCESS: Public tours are available.

inherit—to be given someone's property after they die

DANVERS STATE HOSPITAL

Danvers State Hospital was built in the 1870s to care for the mentally ill. The hospital grew to include more than 40 buildings. It was built to hold 600 patients, but by 1945 it had as many as 2,360 patients. Not much was known then about treating mental illness. Harsh methods were used to keep the patients under control. Some people believe this treatment led the ghosts of the hospital's patients to haunt the property today.

The 2001 horror film *Session 9* was filmed at Danvers State Hospital before the building was torn down.

Jeralyn Levasseur grew up on the property. Her father was the hospital administrator. She remembers unexplained footsteps in their house, lights flickering, and doors opening and closing on their own. One day she saw the ghost of a woman in the attic. Another day the covers on her bed were pulled off when no one else was in the room.

Stories like Levasseur's drew ghost hunters and tourists to Danvers after the hospital closed in 1992. Many visitors left believing the building was haunted. Today most of the former hospital has been torn down. The only buildings that remain have been turned into luxury apartments, leaving the hauntings of Danvers State Hospital a mystery.

CITY: Danvers, Massachusetts

DATE OF FIRST REPORTED HAUNTING: unknown

TYPES OF ACTIVITY: ghost sightings, ghostly touches, footsteps, moving objects

SCARY RANKING: 4

ACCESS: There is no public access.

U.S.S. CONSTELLATION

CITY: Baltimore, Maryland

FIRST REPORTED HAUNTING: 1955

TYPES OF ACTIVITY: ghost sightings, strange smells, noises, unexplained lights

SCARY RANKING: 2

ACCESS: Public tours are available.

The U.S.S. *Constellation* was the first ship built by the U.S. Navy. First launched in 1797, the *Constellation* engaged in several battles. In 1853 the ship was taken apart, and a new ship with the same name was built. For another 100 years, the *Constellation* performed new duties. The ship brought food to Ireland during a **famine**. It was a training site for sailors during World War I (1914–1918). The *Constellation* was taken out of service in 1955. The ship is now a National Historic Landmark in Baltimore, Maryland.

Ghost sightings aboard the *Constellation* started occurring the same year it was taken out of service. Two ghosts, a sailor and a captain, have been seen roaming the decks. Visitors claim they are the ghosts of Captain Thomas Truxton and sailor Neil Harvey. In the 1700s Navy officers used harsh punishments for sailors. In 1799 Truxton ordered that sailor Harvey be killed for falling asleep on watch.

Other ghostly sightings have been reported aboard the *Constellation*. A priest once thanked staff for his well-informed tour guide. He later found out that there was no tour guide. Other visitors have seen ghostly lights and heard unexplained noises on the ship. Often the smell of gunpowder occurs before the **paranormal** events.

"One time, I switched on the alarm system, turned off all the lights and locked up for the night. The next day, the place was still locked from the inside, but the lights and a radio were on."
– James L. Hudgins, director of the U.S.S. *Constellation* in 1976

famine—a serious shortage of food resulting in widespread hunger and death
paranormal—having to do with an event that has no scientific explanation

GOVERNOR SPRAGUE MANSION MUSEUM

CITY: Cranston, Rhode Island

FIRST REPORTED HAUNTING: 1928

TYPES OF ACTIVITY: ghost sightings, footsteps, voices, cold spots, ghostly touches

SCARY RANKING: 4

ACCESS: Open for visitors, weddings, and parties.

At first glance, the Governor Sprague Mansion Museum appears to be an old, stately home. However, its white columns and formal furnishings mask a dark past.

The Sprague Mansion began as a modest home. It was built in Cranston, Rhode Island, in the late 1700s. It takes its name from Colonel Amasa Sprague, who in the 1800s turned the house into an elegant mansion. However, Sprague was murdered on New Year's Eve in 1843. John Gordon, who worked for Sprague, was found guilty of the murder and was executed. However, later evidence suggested Gordon was not guilty.

Today many people think the ghost of John Gordon haunts Sprague Mansion. Visitors have heard footsteps and voices, seen ghosts, and felt pockets of cold air in the house. Some people have seen a woman in black through a window. Others have felt mysterious touches when no one was around.

At least two groups of people said they received strange messages through Ouija boards. One of those messages led visitors to believe a butler named Charlie was haunting the house. They believe his ghost is upset because the mansion owner's son refused to marry Charlie's daughter. Through the Ouija board, Charlie told the visitors, "Tell my story." As a result, every year, the mansion hosts a Halloween party in honor of Charlie. While some claim to feel Charlie's cold touch at the party, Charlie himself has yet to show up.

Halloween at the Governor Sprague Mansion Museum

Real or Fake?

The large number of books, TV shows, and movies about haunted places is evidence of our fascination with the unknown. These stories scare us, thrill us, and help bring history to life. The next time you visit a battlefield, old hotel, or historic building, keep an eye out. You never know what—or whom—you might find beside you.

GHOSTS OF THE
ALAMO
AND OTHER HAUNTINGS
OF THE SOUTH

TABLE OF CONTENTS

Do you believe in ghosts and haunted places? Are the dead walking among us? Some people think so, while others claim haunted places and ghost sightings can be explained. The southern United States is said to have many haunted locations—places where spirits have returned or the dead continue to roam. It's up to you to decide whether the terrors in the South are real.

ST. AUGUSTINE LIGHTHOUSE

The St. Augustine Lighthouse is famous for its hauntings. Legends say that the ghosts are of people who died at the lighthouse. A caretaker of the property hung himself on the porch. Another worker fell to his death from the top of the tower. Three young girls drowned in the waters outside of the lighthouse.

CITY: St. Augustine, Florida

FIRST REPORTED HAUNTING: 1873

TYPES OF ACTIVITY: unexplained voices and footsteps, ghost sightings

SCARY RANKING: 2

ACCESS: Limited tours are available.

Today people claim to have experienced ghostly events at the lighthouse. The laughter of young girls can be heard when no children are there. A ghost that looks like the man who fell is said to roam the property. Some reports involve the **spirit** of the caretaker. He was known to enjoy smoking cigars while on duty. Visitors have smelled fresh cigar smoke on the property, even though no one is smoking nearby.

the spiral staircase of the St. Augustine Lighthouse

spirit—the invisible part of a person that contains thoughts and feelings; some people believe the spirit leaves the body after death

THE ALAMO

In 1836 a 13-day battle took place at the Alamo in San Antonio, Texas. Between 800 and 2,000 men were killed in the bloody conflict between Texan fighters and the Mexican army. More than 175 years later, people claim the spirits of the dead roam free at the historic Texas landmark.

The Alamo was originally built in the 1700s as Mission San Antonio de Valero. It was supposed to be a place of worship and religious education. Instead, it became a landmark for the famous standoff. The historic location is open for tours today.

Sightings of the fighters' spirits are commonly reported at the Alamo. A visitor heard voices echoing in one building, yet he knew he was alone. The voices got louder and louder. Finally, one voice called out to the man, "It's too late!" The man left the building and went straight to the Alamo security.

A worker at the Alamo has heard spirits call out. The spirits seem to be carrying out the famous battle. The worker claims to have heard "Fire!" "He's dead!" and "Here they come!" from within the Alamo.

"I noticed a man standing there gazing into the display case ... he was all dressed up in old-fashioned clothing. Then I realized I was looking at a ghost ... I could look right through him." —a visitor to the Alamo

MYRTLES PLANTATION

Myrtles **Plantation** was built more than 200 years ago. Today the plantation is a bed and breakfast, restaurant, and the site of various receptions. But it is also considered one of the most haunted houses in America. Many people have owned the home, and each owner has experienced paranormal activity.

The most famous ghost is Chloe, a young **slave** who was killed on the property. Legend says she poisoned members of the family who lived there. She was hung, and her body was thrown into a river. Visitors to the plantation have claimed to see Chloe in guest rooms and on the grounds. Chloe was missing an ear. Witnesses report seeing Chloe's ghost wearing a green scarf to cover the missing ear. It is said that Chloe steals earrings from guest rooms and pins them on the scarf.

According to visitors, Chloe isn't the only ghost at the plantation. Crying babies are heard when none are in the building. Footsteps echo down empty hallways. **Apparitions** wander in the lobby. Many guests are so terrified they leave in the middle of the night.

CITY: near St. Francisville, Louisiana

FIRST REPORTED HAUNTING: 1950s

TYPES OF ACTIVITY: vanishing objects, strange smells, unexplained footsteps

SCARY RANKING: 2

ACCESS: Tours are offered.

plantation—a large farm where crops such as cotton and sugarcane are grown
slave—a person who is owned by another person; slaves were forced to work without pay
apparition—the visible appearance of a ghost

THE LALAURIE MANSION

New Orleans is a popular vacation spot for tourists, attracting millions of visitors each year. But visitors may not know the legendary paranormal history of the bustling city. In the center is the LaLaurie Mansion, also known as Hell House. Delphine LaLaurie lived in the mansion and was known to abuse her slaves. She once chased a young slave across the roof of the home with a whip. The girl jumped to her death and was buried on the property.

CITY: New Orleans, Louisiana

FIRST REPORTED HAUNTING: 1834

TYPES OF ACTIVITY: ghostly screams, unexplained noises

SCARY RANKING: 4

ACCESS: The mansion is privately owned and not open for tours.

The true horror of Hell House was uncovered in 1834 when the home caught fire. When firefighters came to the house, they found slaves trapped in the attic. Some of the slaves were living in cages, while others were chained to the wall. Many had been beaten nearly to death. A few slaves were rescued, but most of them died.

Many people have owned the home since the LaLauries fled the city after the fire. Owners, visitors, and guests of the home have reported ghostly sightings. The ghost of Delphine has been seen wandering through the home. Bloodcurdling screams have been reported in the attic. The slave who fell to her death has been spotted wandering in the yard. People have reported strange sounds, such as screaming and cracking whips, coming from empty rooms. One resident of the home claimed to have been attacked by a man shackled in chains.

BELL WITCH CAVE

The Bell Witch Cave in Tennessee was named after a spirit that supposedly haunted the area. But the hauntings didn't begin in the cave. Starting in 1817, John Bell and his family were haunted by a ghost that became known as the Bell Witch of Tennessee. Bell was a wealthy farmer who owned a great deal of land. The property was where the witch terrorized the Bell family and anyone who visited the farm.

CITY: Adams, Tennessee

FIRST REPORTED HAUNTING: 1817

TYPES OF ACTIVITY: strange noises, apparitions, unexplained death

SCARY RANKING: 5

ACCESS: Public tours of the cave and the property are available.

The haunting of Bell Farm became well known because of the Bell Witch's reported aggressive behavior. The witch was believed to be responsible for injuring several members of the family. The family heard strange noises and knocks at the door when no one was there. Scratching and clawing sounds were heard at night with no explanation. Then the children began to be attacked while they slept. Their hair was violently pulled, and their covers were ripped from their beds. Yet when they awoke, they were alone.

the home of John Bell

The Bell Witch is said to have communicated with family members and visitors to the farm. Many people reported speaking directly with the witch. She seemed to be very angry with the family, especially John Bell. "I'll keep after him until the end of his days!" the witch reportedly told visitors to the Bell Farm. "Old Jack Bell's days are numbered." According to legend, the witch kept her promise. She was blamed for murdering John Bell by poisoning him while he slept.

Today the home is no longer standing on the property. However, visitors can take a tour of the Bell Witch Cave and the land where the Bell Witch terrorized the family. Tourists have reported strange and unexplained occurrences in the cave. One woman claimed to see the ghost of a woman floating across the cave entrance.

After John died, his family found a vial of fluid. They realized John had been poisoned after giving some of the fluid to the cat, which died.

"It had the complete figure of a person [until] it got down to about its ankles. It wasn't touching the floor at all. It was just drifting ... bouncing along."
– Bill Eden, former owner of the land describing a ghost he saw

WAVERLY HILLS SANATORIUM

The original Waverly Hills **Sanatorium** was built in 1910, but it was remodeled from 1924 to 1926 and reopened. The new building was used as a hospital for people suffering from the deadly disease **tuberculosis**. But what was supposed to be a place for medical treatment soon became a terrifying location.

Thousands of patients died at Waverly. The facility had a 500-foot (152-meter) tunnel used to carry supplies in and out of the sanatorium. Eventually, the dead were transported to the bottom of the property through the tunnel. It became known as the "body chute" or "death tunnel," and it was the scene of many ghostly occurrences.

CITY: Louisville, Kentucky

FIRST REPORTED HAUNTING: 1962

TYPES OF ACTIVITY: Unexplained noises, ghostly sightings

SCARY RANKING: 4

ACCESS: Tours are available, including private overnight tours.

When scientists found a cure for tuberculosis, the hospital closed. But some of its patients may have stayed behind. Visitors and workers have heard unexplained voices and screams of terror. People claim to see a ghost of an old woman who stands at the front door, begging visitors for help. The voice of a former patient has been heard screaming "Get out!" to anyone who comes near the building.

Room 502 is one of the most haunted locations in the building. Two hospital workers killed themselves there. Decades after they died, ghosts reportedly haunted visitors in the room. Strange voices are heard saying, "Remember me?"

Many paranormal investigators have visited Waverly Hills. One group claimed to make contact with a ghost in Room 502. Other groups have claimed to have gotten **EVP** recordings of ghosts at Waverly.

sanatorium—a place for the care and treatment of people recovering from illness
tuberculosis—a disease caused by bacteria that causes fever, weight loss, and coughing; left untreated, tuberculosis can lead to death
EVP—sounds or voices heard during electronic recordings that can't be explained; EVP stands for electronic voice phenomena

MAMMOTH CAVE

The Mammoth Cave in Kentucky is the largest known cave system in the world. It is also considered to be one of the most haunted caves in the world. Settlers originally explored the cave searching for valuable minerals. Mining is dangerous work, and many settlers were killed. Some of the bodies remained in the cave for many years.

Today the cave is part of a national park. Visitors take tours of the cave. Many have reported having paranormal experiences. There have been sightings of ghostly apparitions in the cave. Some of the scariest moments come when the tour guides conduct a "blackout." During a blackout, they turn off the lights. One park guide claimed to have been shoved and heard footsteps when no one was around.

The most famous ghost of Mammoth Cave is Stephen Bishop. He was a former slave who worked in the cave as a guide. For years after his death, visitors reported seeing Bishop's ghost.

A park ranger claimed she had an encounter with a ghost dressed in denim pants and suspenders. At first she thought the ghost was a man following the tour group. But when the guide turned to look for him, the man was no longer with the group. Another guide searched for the man but couldn't find him. The guide thought she must have seen a ghost.

CITY: Mammoth Cave, Kentucky

FIRST REPORTED HAUNTING: early 1800s

TYPES OF ACTIVITY: apparitions, unexplained noises and footsteps

SCARY RANKING: 3

ACCESS: The National Park has regular tours available.

THE BILTMORE HOTEL

The Biltmore Hotel in Florida is a place where the rich and famous used to stay. It is also a place where one **infamous** guest met his end.

Gangster Thomas "Fats" Walsh ran an illegal gambling operation from a suite on the 13th floor. One night in 1929, an angry gambler shot Fats, and the famous gangster died in the bathroom. His blood left a permanent stain on the marble of the bathroom floor.

Walsh's ghost is said to be very active at the hotel. Guests say the elevator skips stops and takes them directly to the 13th floor. When the doors open, Walsh can be heard shouting and screaming.

CITY: Coral Gables, Florida

FIRST REPORTED HAUNTING: 1960s

TYPES OF ACTIVITY: ghosts, unexplained noises, objects moving

SCARY RANKING: 5

ACCESS: The hotel is still in operation.

Witnesses have reported seeing many other ghosts at the Biltmore. Most of the ghosts are said to be friendly. A dishwasher claimed he saw the ghost of a man dressed in a top hat playing the piano. He might have been playing music for the ghostly couples sometimes spotted in the ballroom dancing. Witnesses say they were dressed in old-fashioned clothing and were **transparent**. Another ghost is said to appear on the 13th floor of the Biltmore. One guest said the ghost greeted her and was very friendly.

infamous—known for a negative act or behavior
transparent—easily seen through

53

THE CRESCENT HOTEL

The Crescent Hotel seemed doomed to be haunted before the first guest arrived. While the hotel was being built in 1884, a worker fell through the roof and died. His body landed where room 218 of the hotel is located today. One guest of room 218 reported waking in the middle of the night being violently shaken. He heard footsteps moving across the room but saw no one. Another guest in the room woke one night to see the walls spattered with blood. She is said to have run from the room screaming. When hotel workers investigated, the walls looked normal.

In the 1930s Norman Baker bought the hotel to open a hospital. According to legend, Baker did experiments on his patients, killing many of them. He eventually went to prison for mail fraud. More than 70 years later, guests have claimed to see the ghost of Baker wandering the halls of the hotel.

The hotel is once again open for guests, and the paranormal reports continue to roll in. Witnesses say a ghost wanders the lobby dressed in formal clothing of the Victorian Era. He never speaks and never bothers anyone. Guests also report doors slamming and other ghost sightings. One of the most terrifying accounts happened when a family in room 424 was watching TV. Suddenly an apparition walked through the closed and locked door. It wandered across the room and into the bathroom. The terrified family fled the Crescent and never returned.

CITY: Eureka Springs, Arkansas

FIRST REPORTED HAUNTING: 1937

TYPES OF ACTIVITY: ghost sightings, unexplained noises

SCARY RANKING: 4

ACCESS: The hotel and spa are still in operation; ghost tours are available.

MOUNDSVILLE PENITENTIARY

Moundsville **Penitentiary** in West Virginia was shut down in 1995. But for more than 100 years, it held some of the most violent prisoners in the country. More than 1,000 men died inside the walls of Moundsville. Many were hung or electrocuted for their crimes. Others were beaten to death in prison riots. Some died in fights between inmates living in horrible, overcrowded conditions.

Guards, inmates, and visitors have reported strange events at the prison since the 1930s. Unexplained noises, freezing cold spots in the middle of summer, and ghostly apparitions are part of the prison **lore**.

One of the most infamous murders in the prison occurred in 1929. R.D. Wall was an inmate at Moundsville. Three new inmates saw him talking to guards one day. The inmates later cornered Wall and brutally attacked him. Since then there have been many sightings of a ghost—possibly Wall—wandering the maintenance area of the prison.

CITY: Moundsville, West Virginia

FIRST REPORTED HAUNTING: as early as the 1930s; many reports began in the 1990s after the prison was closed

TYPES OF ACTIVITY: ghost sightings, unexplained voices, footsteps, and screams

SCARY RANKING: 3

ACCESS: Guided tours are available, including overnight stays.

penitentiary—a prison for people found guilty of serious crimes
lore—a collection of knowledge and traditions of a particular
group that has been passed down over generations

One of the scariest reports involves a headless ghost seen wandering the halls. Many people think the ghost is Frank Hyer, an inmate who was hanged at Moundsville in 1931. He was the last of 94 prisoners who were executed at the penitentiary.

The prison is open for tours, and brave souls can even spend the night in one of the cells. Many people report hearing unexplained noises and feeling sudden cold chills. There are regular sightings of orbs and ghostly apparitions.

"There was something like a light bar moving around ... like it was walking back and forth, pacing at the top of the stairs, which led to the basement of the penitentiary."
– a tour worker at Moundsville

Hauntings: Fact or Fiction?

Do the spirits of the dead haunt the hotels, houses, and other buildings of the South? Or are there logical explanations behind the encounters? Whether you're a believer or a **skeptic**, you may want to leave the lights on if you visit these places!

skeptic—a person who questions things that other people believe in

BACHELOR'S GROVE
CEMETERY
AND OTHER HAUNTED PLACES
OF THE MIDWEST

TABLE OF CONTENTS

From hotels to restaurants, the midwestern United States is filled with haunted places. People have reported thousands of spooky encounters with the dead. Are there logical explanations for these sightings? Or is the heartland of America home to some of the scariest ghosts in the world? Dare to read on and decide for yourself!

FRANKLIN CASTLE

The sight of the Franklin Castle can send shivers down anyone's spine. The 28-room stone castle has a **Gothic** look. According to legend, many murders and deaths have happened at the castle over the last 100 years.

Some people think the castle is haunted by those who died there. A young girl was killed in a secret passageway. Another girl was murdered in her bed. Owners of the home once found a collection of baby skeletons hidden in a secret room. Visitors and past owners have reported hearing crying babies when none were present.

The original owner of the castle was a man named Hannes Tiedemann. He supposedly murdered a woman in the castle. Many people have reported seeing "the woman in black." She is an apparition that sits in the tower of the castle looking out the window.

CITY: Cleveland, Ohio

FIRST REPORTED HAUNTING: 1930s

TYPES OF ACTIVITY: a baby crying, the ghost of a woman in black, doors exploding from the hinges

SCARY RANKING: 3

ACCESS: The castle is privately owned; tours are not available.

Hannes Tiedemann (left) with his wife, Louise, and their son, August

Gothic—in the style of art or architecture used in western Europe between the 1100s and 1500s

BACHELOR'S GROVE CEMETERY

There are few places more creepy than a cemetery after dark. Bachelor's Grove Cemetery in the Bremen Township in Illinois is no exception. It is considered to be one of the most haunted cemeteries in the United States. The last body was buried in Bachelor's Grove in 1989, but the cemetery gets plenty of visitors. There have been more than 100 reported paranormal events on the grounds since 1864.

Ghostly tales from Bachelor's include apparitions that have been seen wandering the graveyard. People have claimed to see the ghost of a woman carrying a baby. The woman wanders throughout the cemetery without a particular direction. When people approach her, she disappears.

CITY: Bremen, Illinois

FIRST REPORTED HAUNTING: 1860s

TYPES OF ACTIVITY: ghostly apparitions, unexplained glowing balls of light

SCARY RANKING: 4

ACCESS: The cemetery is open to the public.

"As I looked up, I saw the deceased woman's husband standing there ... I looked back down in the open grave and then looked back up and they were gone."

—a gravedigger at Bachelor's Grove Cemetery

The most famous ghost of Bachelor's Grove was first seen in the 1970s by two park rangers. They spotted a ghostly figure of a horse emerging from a pond outside the cemetery. The horse was pulling a plow with the ghost of an old man steering it. Legend says that in the 1800s, a farmer drowned in the pond when his horse dragged him in. The pond is also said to hold the bodies of people murdered during the **Prohibition.**

Another ghostly tale from Bachelor's involves a spooky creature. There is a story of a two-headed monster that has been seen running through the cemetery. There have even been paranormal events reported outside the cemetery. People have reported phantom cars on the nearby road that suddenly disappear.

Some people think that the hauntings in Bachelor's Grove Cemetery became more frequent after the rise of **vandalism** in the 1960s. Vandals knocked over tombstones and covered them in spray paint. Some vandals even broke into the graves and stole the bodies. Bones of the dead were found scattered across the cemetery.

the pond at Bachelor's
Grove Cemetery

Prohibition—a time between 1920 and 1933 when it was
illegal to make or sell alcohol in the United States
vandalism—the wrecking of property

BIOGRAPH THEATRE

John Dillinger was a bank robber in the early 1930s. He murdered at least 10 people during his crime spree. The Federal Bureau of Investigation (FBI) searched for Dillinger in 1934. FBI agents eventually tracked him down in Chicago, Illinois, on July 22, 1934. They approached him as he was leaving the Biograph Theatre. When confronted, he ran toward an alley. The agents shot and killed him.

Hauntings have been reported in the 80 years since Dillinger was killed. A ghost of a man matching the gangster's description has been seen outside the theater. Some witnesses have seen him in the alley, running away from the Biograph. The figure then collapses, just as Dillinger did the night he was shot by the FBI. Other visitors report cold spots and odd temperature changes inside the theater. Many have said they feel an unexplained sense of fear when walking past the alley.

John Dillinger

People crowded around the front of the Biograph Theatre after John Dillinger was shot in 1934.

LEMP MANSION

The Lemp family earned a fortune brewing beer, but the family suffered several tragedies. The family **patriarch**, William Lemp, fatally shot himself in his bedroom in the mansion in 1904. Eighteen years later, his son William Jr. carried out the same act in the office. His sister Elsa and brother Charles followed the same fate.

The mansion was sold, and it was turned into a boarding house and eventually a restaurant. During construction, workers reported terrifying paranormal events. Doors slammed with no explanation. The workers often had tools disappear. They also described feeling like they were being watched. Some refused to finish the work. They were too scared to return to Lemp Mansion.

Eventually the work was completed, but the strange events continued. There have been reports of drinking glasses flying through the air and a piano playing with no one seated in front of it. Dinner guests have seen apparitions and heard strange, unexplained noises.

CITY: St. Louis, Missouri

FIRST REPORTED HAUNTING: 1940s

TYPES OF ACTIVITY: ghost sightings, unexplained noises

SCARY RANKING: 4

ACCESS: The mansion is now a restaurant; they also offer haunted tours.

"At about 3:30 a.m., I was in bed asleep and the springs on the bed started pinging as if someone was under the bed pulling and letting go. I jumped out of bed and [ran] into the hall. I only went back when daylight broke and then only slept on the couch."
—a guest staying at the Lemp Mansion in 1994

patriarch—the male leader of a family

GRAND OPERA HOUSE

You might think of ghosts as terrifying, and the thought of seeing one could send shivers down your spine. But the actors and workers at the Grand Opera House say their spirits are friendly.

The Iowa theater has been the site of hauntings for more than 80 years. Many actors like to practice when the theater is empty, which seems to set the stage for ghostly encounters.

Many of the paranormal events at the Grand are similar to those of other haunted places. Doors open and close with no explanation, and lights turn on and off by themselves. Floorboards creak when no one is walking on them. But it is the voices and ghosts that make the haunting of the Grand famous.

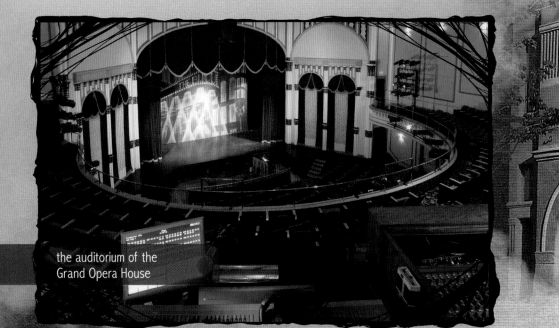
the auditorium of the Grand Opera House

CITY: Dubuque, Iowa

FIRST REPORTED HAUNTING: 1928

TYPES OF ACTIVITY: strange noises, piano music, cold spots

SCARY RANKING: 1

ACCESS: The Grand Opera House was reopened as a theatre with live performances open to the public.

Actors on stage have reported seeing a group of ghosts sitting in the back of the theater. The actors say the ghosts were wearing clothes from long ago. Other actors have reported mysterious voices and singing on stage. In each instance, the theater was empty.

HANNAH HOUSE

CITY: Indianapolis, Indiana

FIRST REPORTED HAUNTING: 1960s

TYPES OF ACTIVITY: unexplained smells coming from an upstairs bedroom, breaking glass in the basement, doors opening on their own, voices in empty rooms

SCARY RANKING: 1

ACCESS: The house is open for tours and events such as wedding receptions.

So much of what makes a haunted house scary can be the building itself. Old Gothic mansions with lots of rooms, basements, and attics leave plenty of space for paranormal guests. One such house, the Hannah House, sits in the heart of Indianapolis. The home was built in 1858, but the first ghosts weren't reported until about 100 years later. People believe two of the spirits are the original owners, wealthy politician Alexander Moore Hannah and his wife, Elizabeth.

Visitors passing by the second floor bedroom have had strange experiences. They reported that the door to the room swung open on its own. Some have smelled rotting flesh coming from within the room. Elizabeth Hannah's baby was delivered in that room, but it wasn't alive. Some people say the room is haunted with death.

the second floor bedroom

The basement of the Hannah House is another hot spot for paranormal activity. Alexander Hannah was reportedly associated with the Underground Railroad. According to legend, tragedy struck one night when a group of slaves seeking freedom stopped at his house. As the slaves slept in the basement, a lamp was accidentally tipped over, which set off a massive blaze. The slaves died. Hannah then buried the bodies under the basement's dirt floor to cover up the fact that he had been protecting slaves. Visitors and workers have reported crashing, breaking glass, and other odd noises coming from the basement.

One ghost that supposedly haunts the Hannah House is described as "grandfatherly." Some visitors have said the well-dressed man simply disappeared before their eyes. Others, including the granddaughter of a couple living in the home, claimed to have conversations with the ghost. Those who have encountered him describe him as a friendly ghost.

STEPP FAMILY CEMETERY

Like Bachelor's Grove, Stepp Cemetery is a small, out-of-the-way cemetery. No one has been buried there in years. But there is one grave—the grave of a small child—that is said to be haunted.

Legend says the ghost of an old woman sits on a stump next to the child's grave every night. The stump is shaped like a chair, and the ghost keeps watch over the grave.

There are various stories behind the ghost of Stepp Cemetery. The most common story is of a ghostly mother watching over her daughter who is buried in the grave. The daughter was hit by a car and killed, and the mother had the tree cut down to form a permanent seat. Some versions of the story say the woman has put a **curse** on the stump. Anyone who sits on the stump will die exactly one year later.

CITY: Martinsville, Indiana

FIRST REPORTED HAUNTING: 1950s

TYPES OF ACTIVITY: the ghost of a woman near the grave of a young child

SCARY RANKING: 2

ACCESS: The cemetery and surrounding woods are open to the public.

STEPP CEMETERY

ESTABLISHED EARLY 1800's

curse—an evil spell meant to harm someone

ASHMORE ESTATES

CITY: Ashmore, Illinois

FIRST REPORTED HAUNTING: 1970s

TYPES OF ACTIVITY: ghosts and unexplained noises

SCARY RANKING: 1

ACCESS: Ghost tours are available at Ashmore Estates, including overnight stays.

Ashmore Estates was built in 1916 on farmland in Illinois. Originally called the Coles County Poor Farm, it housed people who were poor and needed help. But living conditions at the farm were bad. An estimated 200 people died on the farm. They were buried in a cemetery on the property. The dead included a young girl who was burned in a fire in 1880. Her name was Elva Skinner, and legend says that she haunts Ashmore Estates to this day.

The property was sold in 1959 and was used as a mental hospital until it was closed in 1987. The building was abandoned and became the target of vandals. It was then that the stories of ghosts at Ashmore began to increase. Reports of floating ghosts and unexplained noises at Ashmore spread through the small community. Visitors claimed to hear voices coming from empty rooms. Many people believe that the spirits of those who died on the land are responsible for the hauntings.

"I felt like something was trying to pull me off the floor."
– TV meteorologist Kevin Orpurt describing his stay at the Ashmore Estates

THE GREAT LAKES

LOCATION: The five **Great Lakes** in the Midwest

FIRST REPORTED HAUNTING: 1600s

TYPES OF ACTIVITY: ghost ships sailing years after they sank, apparitions of dead sailors

SCARY RANKING: 1

ACCESS: Most shipwrecks are open to divers for exploration.

The Great Lakes have swallowed more than 6,000 ships and serve as a watery grave for more than 100,000 men. The spirits of the dead are said to live on in the depths of the lakes. But some people believe the ghosts aren't the only things haunting the waters.

The Ghost of "Grandpa"

A dead body on land will quickly **decompose**, but a dead body in icy cold water can be preserved for decades. The SS *Kamloops* sank in 270 feet (82 m) of water off the coast of Michigan in 1927. Divers exploring the wreckage have reported the ghostly corpse of an old sailor trapped within the ship. Nicknamed "grandpa," the ghost is said to be stuck in the engine room of the ship. Divers say that grandpa follows them as they explore the wreckage. Some say it is the spirit of the old man who died when the ship went down. Others say the body simply floats because the divers are stirring up the water.

Great Lakes—a group of five connected freshwater lakes that lie along the border between the United States and Canada; they are Lakes Superior, Michigan, Huron, Erie and Ontario

decompose—to rot or decay

The *Edmund Fitzgerald* was a huge cargo ship that sank in a terrible storm in Lake Superior in 1975. All 29 men on board went down with the ship. One body was found during an exploration dive to the wreckage in 1994, but the other bodies were never recovered. But there have been several sightings of the *Fitzgerald* since 1975. Crews have reported seeing the ship sailing where it was last spotted before it sank. The shattered ship remains 530 feet (162 m) below the surface, so how is it possible that people have seen it gliding on the water?

the wreckage of the *Edmund Fitzgerald*

The *Fitzgerald* is just one of hundreds of ghost sightings on the Great Lakes. The first documented ship to sink on the Great Lakes was the *Griffon*, a French supply ship. The *Griffon* was lost on the waters of Lake Michigan in September 1679. For more than 300 years sailors have reported seeing the ghost ship of the *Griffon*. A heavy fog sometimes rolls across the lake. Some visitors have claimed to see the ship emerging from the fog and suddenly vanishing.

GHOSTS OF ALCATRAZ
AND OTHER HAUNTINGS
OF THE WEST

TABLE OF CONTENTS

Nearly every town has a legend about a haunted place. Maybe it's the creepy house on the corner, where a lone figure watches from a second-story window. Perhaps it's the high school auditorium, where the ghost of a former student wanders the stage. Whether or not we believe in ghosts, these stories have the power to haunt us. The United States is home to some of the world's creepiest haunted places. Take a tour of the western United States and explore its stories of ghosts and hauntings.

ALCATRAZ ISLAND

One of the most famous haunted places in the United States is Alcatraz prison. Even before the famous prison was built, Alcatraz Island in California was said to be haunted. According to legend, the Miwok Indians thought evil spirits lived there. Historians think the Miwok sent tribe members there to punish them for breaking laws.

CITY: Alcatraz Island, California

FIRST REPORTED HAUNTING: 1963, maybe earlier

TYPES OF ACTIVITY: screams, crying, music, cold spots

SCARY RANKING: 5

ACCESS: Guided and self-guided tours are available through the National Park Service.

After California became a state in 1850, the federal government built a military fortress on Alcatraz to guard the coast. In the 1860s it became a training site for Union soldiers during the Civil War (1861–1865). Around the same time, a military prison opened on the island.

Alcatraz prison was **renovated** by 1912, becoming the world's biggest reinforced concrete building. Eventually, the cost of bringing fresh water, food, and supplies to the island grew too large. The Army closed the prison and left the island in 1933.

The prison became a federal penitentiary in 1934 and was known for its strict security. Many prisoners tried to escape, but there is no evidence that any of them made it out alive. Alcatraz finally closed in 1963.

renovate—to restore something to good condition

Visitation windows sat at the end of a hallway lined with cell blocks

Although Alcatraz closed, many people believe ghosts stayed behind. Since the National Park Service took over the island in 1973, numerous visitors have reported signs of paranormal activity. Tourists hear the clanging of metal and the cries and screams of inmates. Cell 14-D is often noted to be particularly cold, and several visitors have reported feeling strong emotions inside. The cell held a single prisoner who had no contact with other people for more than three years.

One of Alcatraz's most famous inmates was the gangster Al Capone. He was reported to frequently play the banjo in the prison's shower room. Today visitors report the ghostly sounds of a banjo lingering in the showers.

Al Capone

The paranormal events at Alcatraz have enticed visitors to the island. Some visitors believe the same goes for both ghosts and former prisoners—no one can escape from Alcatraz.

STANLEY HOTEL

Brothers Francis and F. O. Stanley made a fortune after inventing a steam-powered car, the Stanley Steamer. F. O. took his wealth and moved to Estes Park, Colorado. He built the Stanley Hotel, a resort with stunning views of the Rocky Mountains and nearby valleys. It offered guests many activities, including bowling, golf, and orchestra concerts. Guests included former U.S. President Theodore Roosevelt, musician Bob Dylan, and writer Stephen King. King found the hotel to be unsettling and creepy, which inspired him to write his famous book *The Shining*.

King isn't the only one to have felt uneasy at the Stanley Hotel, which is still open today. Guests have reported having their feet tickled during the night and having their luggage mysteriously unpacked. Lights turn on and off by themselves, and children's voices are heard in empty halls. Some visitors have seen the ghost of F. O. walking in the lobby.

CITY: Estes Park, Colorado

FIRST REPORTED HAUNTING: 1950s

TYPES OF ACTIVITY: ghost sightings, voices, ghostly touches, moving objects

SCARY RANKING: 3

ACCESS: Several tour options are available, including history tours and ghost hunt tours; the hotel also takes overnight guests.

Most people who say they've encountered the ghosts believe they're friendly. Some people think the Stanleys and their original staff want to make sure guests have a pleasant stay.

QUEEN MARY SHIP

CITY: Long Beach, California

FIRST REPORTED HAUNTING: 1967

TYPES OF ACTIVITY: ghost sightings, voices, smells, moving objects

SCARY RANKING: 5

ACCESS: Many tour options are available.

After the *Queen Mary* ship was built in the 1930s, it carried movie stars and British royalty between Europe and North America. During World War II (1939–1945), it was briefly painted gray and used to transport soldiers. It then returned to its job of transporting passengers. The *Queen Mary* was bigger than the famous passenger ship *Titanic*, and it was called the most glamorous ship ever built. It stopped running in 1967 after its owners lost too much business to airplane travel.

"The Queen Mary is the most haunted place that I have ever investigated, and I've literally been around the globe with hauntings ... There are at least 600 active resident ghosts on the Queen Mary."
– Peter James, famous psychic

Today the ship is docked in Long Beach, California. It is used as a hotel and party **venue**. However, its long history seems to have left a few ghosts behind. At one point during the war, the *Queen Mary* crashed into another ship and split it in two. Today visitors report hearing a loud collision and the cries of drowning sailors.

There are also reports of ghosts from the ship's passenger days. Visitors have heard the voice of a young girl who drowned in one of the ship's pools. Staff members have seen waves in the pool and wet footprints near it at night after the pool is locked. Staff members have also seen ghosts of people dressed in old clothing. Workers have even reported **poltergeist** activity, such as plates flying across the room, pictures moving, and doors opening and closing.

Cabin class passengers would gather at one of the lounges for a marvelous view over the bow of the *Queen Mary*.

venue—the place where an event happens
poltergeist—a ghost that causes physical events, like objects moving

WHALEY HOUSE

Thomas Whaley built the Whaley House in San Diego in 1857. It was one of the finest houses in Southern California. However, the Whaley House was the site of tragedy and death. One of Thomas' sons died at 17 months, and one of his daughters killed herself. Legal problems led to Thomas losing all his money. He became bitter and mean, dying in 1890 at age 67.

"I heard the heavy footsteps upstairs when nobody was there but me. It sounded just like there was somebody else in the house. I heard moving around in a closet and everything, but there was nobody there."
– a docent for the Whaley House

Today the Whaley House is a museum where visitors can learn about the area's history and the building's ghostly encounters. Many people believe the house is haunted by its tragic past. According to the Whaley House's **docent**, even Thomas Whaley heard mysterious heavy footsteps in the house. Whaley believed that Yankee Jim, an accused thief who had been hanged on the property, was haunting him. Many people think Thomas Whaley and his family haunt the house too. Some have claimed to see the ghost of the Whaleys' infant son.

Visitors have reported various types of strange activity. They claimed to experience cold spots, unexplained lights, and noises with no source. Other visitors have reported hearing phantom piano music and the feeling of people brushing up against them when no one is nearby. One docent saw a room filled with fog that couldn't be explained. Some visitors reported seeing the ghost of a man hanging in a doorway.

docent—a guide at a museum, art gallery, or zoo

THORNEWOOD CASTLE

CITY: Lakewood, Washington

FIRST REPORTED HAUNTING: 2000

TYPES OF ACTIVITY: ghost sightings, moving objects

SCARY RANKING: 1

ACCESS: The castle is a bed-and-breakfast and wedding venue; tours are sometimes offered.

In 1907 wealthy businessman Chester "Ches" Thorne set out to build his dream home. He had an English castle taken apart and shipped piece by piece to Lakewood, Washington. He used a combination of the old pieces and new materials to put the house back together. U.S. presidents Theodore Roosevelt and William Howard Taft visited the house when it was finished.

Ches died in 1927, but some people think his spirit is still in Thornewood Castle. One of the owners believes his ghost is responsible for many strange experiences. She's seen glass break and lightbulbs come unscrewed without reason. Several people have seen a man—thought to be Ches' ghost—in a riding suit and spurs.

Other spirits have been reported wandering Thornewood Castle. Women getting married at the castle have looked in a mirror and seen the image of a woman wearing clothing from the early 1900s. A ghostly woman has been seen looking out a window from the same room.

THE ALASKAN HOTEL

A gold rush brought settlers to Alaska in the late 1800s and early 1900s. In 1913 two brothers built the Alaskan Hotel in Juneau. Miners stayed there between trips into the wild to look for gold. When they found gold, they came back to the hotel to spend it.

Today the Alaskan Hotel & Bar is still open, and it's the longest-operating hotel in the state. Staff and visitors tell many stories of ghostly encounters. Local stories say that a woman, murdered by her jealous husband, haunts the hotel. The hotel's front desk clerk says that Room 219 is always cold. Guests frequently ask to be moved out of the room. Other guests have reported seeing the ghost of a woman who touches them or sits on their beds. Housekeepers say they have put a stack of towels down in one place, only to find them mysteriously appear somewhere else later.

CITY: Juneau, Alaska

FIRST REPORTED HAUNTING: unknown

TYPES OF ACTIVITY: ghost sightings, cold spots, moving objects, ghostly touches

SCARY RANKING: 2

ACCESS: The hotel is open to the public.

BIG NOSE KATE'S SALOON

CITY: Tombstone, Arizona

FIRST REPORTED HAUNTING: unknown

TYPES OF ACTIVITY: ghost sightings, moving objects, mysterious footsteps, ghostly touches

SCARY RANKING: 4

ACCESS: The restaurant and bar are open to the public.

The gunfight at the O.K. Corral is one of the most famous in U.S. history. The event took place in 1881 in Tombstone, Arizona Territory, between lawmen and bandits. Before the gunfight, the bandits stayed at the Grand Hotel in Tombstone. The hotel burned down in 1882 and was replaced by Big Nose Kate's Saloon, which is still open today.

Visitors to Big Nose Kate's have spotted the apparitions of bandits. They've been seen perched on bar stools and spilling drinks in the basement. Guests have had their hair pulled and seen chairs and bar stools move without being touched. Lights turn on and off, and boot steps echo across the dance floor. Bartenders count the number of glasses that fly across the room without being touched. The ghost of an old miner nicknamed "Swamper" has also been seen throughout the building. Legends say he buried silver in the building and has stayed to protect it.

"I've had them [ghosts] yank my hair back, touch me, walk by me when there's no one there. Chairs beside me move like someone just walked up and pulled out a chair to sit down."
– Tricia Rawson, Tombstone tour guide

WINCHESTER MYSTERY HOUSE

CITY: San Jose, California

FIRST REPORTED HAUNTING: 1884

TYPES OF ACTIVITY: ghost sightings, ghostly voices and music, balls of light, strange smells

SCARY RANKING: 4

ACCESS: The house is open daily for tours.

The Winchester Mystery House is an impressive structure, but it has an eerie past. The house's creator, Sarah Pardee, married William Wirt Winchester in 1862 in New Haven, Connecticut. William's father owned the gun company that made the popular Henry Repeater. It was a gun sometimes used by the Union army during the American Civil War. The Henry Repeater made the Winchesters rich, but nothing could protect them from tragedy. In 1866 Sarah gave birth to a daughter who lived only a few days. Fifteen years later, William died of tuberculosis.

Sarah never recovered from the losses of her daughter and husband. A medium told Sarah she was cursed by the ghosts of soldiers, American Indians, and others killed by her husband's rifles. The medium said she should head west and build a home for all the ghosts. Sarah followed the advice.

In 1884 Sarah moved from Connecticut to California and bought an eight-room home in San Jose. She then decided to expand the house. She thought that it would confuse the ghosts, making it hard for them to reach her.

Sarah Winchester

Sarah's bedroom

For the next 38 years, the house was under constant construction. Sarah built staircases that led to nowhere and hallways that doubled back on themselves. She added rooms with no plan or purpose. She built dozens of chimneys so the ghosts could come and go. Sarah lived in the house as a **recluse** until her death in 1922. At that point, the house had about 160 rooms.

Sarah Winchester wasn't the only person to believe the house is filled with ghosts. Since Sarah's death, visitors to the house have reported many eerie encounters. They have seen mysterious balls of light and the ghosts of a gray-haired woman and a workman wearing coveralls. Visitors have also heard phantom voices, ghostly music, and slamming doors. They've even smelled freshly cooked soup in kitchens that haven't been used for decades.

recluse—a person who lives alone and avoids other people

JEROME GRAND HOTEL

The Jerome Grand Hotel had a long history before it became a hotel in 1994. It was originally built in 1926 as a hospital that served Jerome, Arizona. When mining ended in the city in 1950, the hospital closed. The building sat empty for decades.

As soon as the hospital was turned into a hotel in 1994, ghost reports began flooding in. Visitors have seen the ghost of a nurse wandering around the hotel. They've also seen the ghost of a woman who roams the halls and asks for help finding her lost baby. Guests report hearing wheezing, coughs, and voices. Some visitors have felt a child's hand touch them. Others have seen the apparition of a small boy and reported the smell of a hospital. Guests have also been pinched and felt mysterious weights on their beds at night. Many people believe the hotel will forever be haunted by those who died there when it was a hospital.

CITY: Jerome, Arizona

FIRST REPORTED HAUNTING: 1994

TYPES OF ACTIVITY: ghost sightings, voices, smells, ghostly touches

SCARY RANKING: 5

ACCESS: Ghost tours are available.

"The most common occurrence is the sound of labored breathing and coughing coming from empty rooms. Worse, these sounds often **emanate** from a dark corner of a guest's room."
– Southwest Ghost Hunters Association, describing a 2005 study at the hotel

emanate—to spread out from a source

ROOSEVELT HOTEL

CITY: Hollywood, California

FIRST REPORTED HAUNTING: 1985

TYPES OF ACTIVITY: ghost sightings, cold spots, lights turning on and off

SCARY RANKING: 4

ACCESS: The hotel is open to the public.

The Roosevelt Hotel opened in 1927 as a hotel for glamorous Hollywood film stars. The first Academy Awards ceremony was held at the Roosevelt in 1929. Marilyn Monroe lived there for two years at the start of her modeling career. Other movie stars from the 1930s and 1940s, such as Clark Gable and Carole Lombard, also stayed at the Roosevelt.

Today the rich and famous continue to stay at the Roosevelt. However, the hotel is known for more than its star guests. Visitors began to report paranormal events in 1985 after the hotel was renovated. Staff and visitors have claimed to see Marilyn Monroe's face in a mirror. Some guests have seen the ghost of Hollywood star Montgomery Clift pacing in the hallway. The ghost of Carole Lombard, who died at age 33 in a plane crash in 1942, has also been spotted. One guest even brought a Ouija board to the hotel to try to contact Montgomery Clift. She left at 4:00 a.m. in a panic after her room's lights and coffee pot turned themselves on and off.

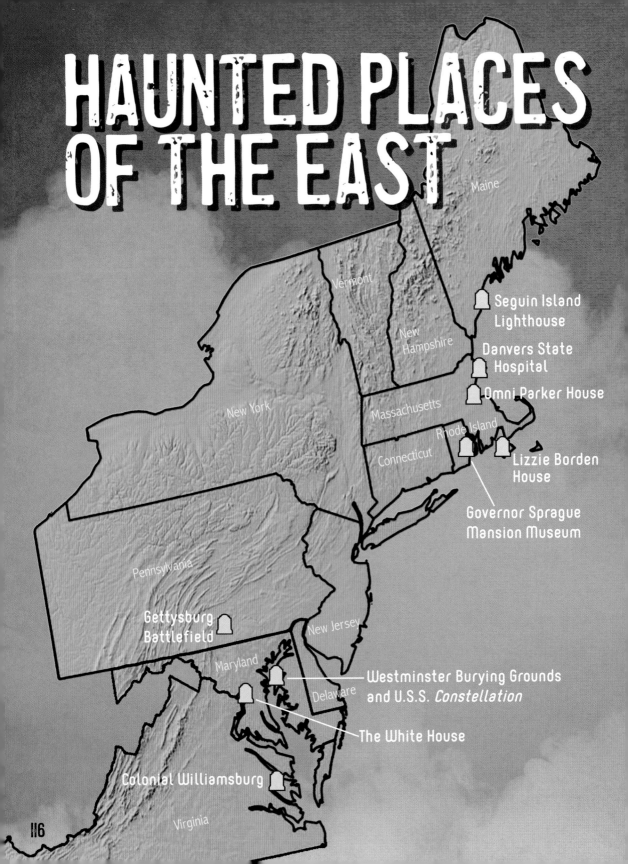

HAUNTED PLACES OF THE EAST

Maine

Vermont

New Hampshire

Seguin Island Lighthouse

Danvers State Hospital

Omni Parker House

New York

Massachusetts

Rhode Island

Connecticut

Lizzie Borden House

Governor Sprague Mansion Museum

Pennsylvania

New Jersey

Gettysburg Battlefield

Maryland

Delaware

Westminster Burying Grounds and U.S.S. *Constellation*

The White House

Colonial Williamsburg

Virginia

OTHER HAUNTED LOCATIONS

- America's Stonehenge in Salem, New Hampshire
- Ice House Restaurant in Burlington, Vermont
- Fort Delaware in Delaware City, Delaware
- Roxy Studios in Long Island City, New York
- Barclay Cemetery in Leroy, Pennsylvania
- Ford's Theatre in Washington, D.C.
- Fredericksburg and Spotsylvania National Military Park, Virginia

HAUNTED PLACES OF THE SOUTH

Moundsville Penitentiary

West Virginia

Kentucky

Virginia

Waverly Hills Sanatorium

Mammoth Cave

North Carolina

Bell Witch Cave

Tennessee

The Crescent Hotel

Oklahoma

Arkansas

South Carolina

Alabama

Georgia

Mississippi

Texas

Louisiana

Myrtles Plantation

St. Augustine Lighthouse

The Alamo

The LaLaurie Mansion

Florida

The Biltmore Hotel

OTHER HAUNTED LOCATIONS

- Eliza Thompson House in Savannah, Georgia
- King's Tavern in Natchez, Mississippi
- Hammock House in Beaufort, North Carolina
- Menger Hotel in San Antonio, Texas
- Cedar Grove Inn in Vicksburg, Mississippi
- Catfish Plantation Restaurant in Waxahachie, Texas
- Jameson Inn in Crestview, Florida
- Kehoe House in Savannah, Georgia
- Sweetwater Mansion in Florence, Alabama
- Magnolia Manor in Bolivar, Tennessee
- Old Charleston Jail in Charleston, South Carolina
- Peavey Melody Music in Meridian, Mississippi

HAUNTED PLACES OF THE MIDWEST

The Great Lakes

Minnesota

Wisconsin

Michigan

Grand Opera House

Iowa

Biograph Theatre

Bachelor's Grove Cemetery

Franklin Castle

Illinois

Indiana

Ohio

Hannah House

Ashmore Estates

Stepp Family Cemetery

Lemp Mansion

Missouri

OTHER HAUNTED LOCATIONS

- Willard Library in Evansville, Indiana
- Grand Opera House in Oshkosh, Wisconsin
- Sica Hollow State Park in Lake City, South Dakota
- Milton School in Alton, Illinois
- Mason House Inn in Bentonsport, Iowa
- Terrance Inn in Petoskey, Michigan
- The Palmer House Hotel in Sauk Centre, Minnesota
- Liberty Memorial Building in Bismarck, North Dakota
- Octagon House in Fond Du Lac, Wisconsin
- Mission Point Resort in Mackinac Island, Michigan
- Holly Hotel in Holly, Michigan

HAUNTED PLACES OF THE WEST

Alaska

The Alaskan Hotel

OTHER HAUNTED LOCATIONS

- San Francisco-Oakland Bay Bridge in San Francisco Bay, California
- Mission La Purisima in Lompoc, California
- Hotel del Coronado in Coronado, California
- McMenamin's Grand Lodge in Forest Grove, Oregon
- The Bush House in Index, Washington
- Rutherglen Mansion Bed and Breakfast in Longview, Washington
- USS *Arizona* in Pearl Harbor, Hawaii
- The Hearthstone Inn in Colorado Springs, Colorado
- Old Idaho Penitentiary in Boise, Idaho
- Little Bighorn Battlefield National Monument in Crow Agency, Montana
- Ivy House Inn Bed and Breakfast in Casper, Wyoming

Thornewood Castle

Washington

Montana

Oregon

Idaho

Wyoming

California

Nevada

Alcatraz Island
Winchester Mystery House

Stanley Hotel

Utah

Colorado

Roosevelt Hotel
Queen Mary Ship

Arizona

New Mexico

Whaley House

Jerome Grand Hotel

Big Nose Kate's Saloon

GLOSSARY

apparition (ap-uh-RISH-uhn)—the visible appearance of a ghost

catacomb (CAT-uh-kohm)—an underground cemetery

Confederacy (kuhn-FED-ur-uh-see)—the 11 southern states that left the United States to form the Confederate States of America

curse (KURS)—an evil spell meant to harm someone

decompose (dee-kuhm-POHZ)—to rot or decay

docent (DOE-sent)—a guide at a museum, art gallery, or zoo

emanate (EM-uh-nate)—to spread out from a source

EVP—sounds or voices heard during electronic recordings that can't be explained; EVP stands for electronic voice phenomenon

famine (FA-muhn)—a serious shortage of food resulting in widespread hunger and death

Gothic (GOTH-ik)—in the style of art or architecture used in western Europe between the 1100s and 1500s

Great Lakes (GRAYT LAKES)—a group of five connected freshwater lakes that lie along the border between the United States and Canada; they are Lakes Superior, Michigan, Huron, Erie, and Ontario

infamous (IN-fuh-muhss)—known for a negative act or behavior

inherit (in-HER-it)—to be given someone's property after they die

lore (LORE)—a collection of knowledge and traditions of a particular group that has been passed down over generations

medium (MEE-dee-uhm)—a person who claims to communicate with the spirit world

orb (ORB)—a glowing ball of light that sometimes appears at a reportedly haunted location

paranormal (pair-uh-NOHR-muhl)—having to do with an event that has no scientific explanation

patriarch (PAY-tree-ark)—the male leader of a family

penitentiary (pen-uh-TEN-chur-ee)—a prison for people found guilty of serious crimes

plantation (plan-TAY-shuhn)—a large farm where crops such as cotton and sugarcane are grown

poltergeist (POL-ter-guyst)—a ghost that causes physical events, such as objects moving

Prohibition (pro-huh-BISH-uhn)—a time between 1920 and 1933 when it was illegal to make or sell alcohol in the United States

recluse (REK-loose)—a person who lives alone and avoids other people

renovate (REH-no-vate)—to restore something to good condition

sanatorium (san-uh-TOR-ee-uhm)—a place for the care and treatment of people recovering from illness

skeptic (SKEP-tik)—a person who questions things that other people believe in

slave (SLAYV)—a person who is owned by another person; slaves were forced to work without pay

spirit (SPIHR-it)—the invisible part of a person that contains thoughts and feelings; some people believe the spirit leaves the body after death

transparent (transs-PAIR-uhnt)—easily seen through

tuberculosis (tu-BUR-kyoo-low-sis)—a disease caused by bacteria that causes fever, weight loss, and coughing; left untreated, tuberculosis can lead to death

Union (YOON-yuhn)—the northern states that fought against the southern states in the Civil War

vandalism (VAN-duhl-izhm)—the wrecking of property

venue (VEN-yoo)—the place where an event happens

INDEX